GET INTO MINECRAFT ®™

GET-INTO-IT GUIDES

VIC KOVACS

CRABTREE
Publishing Company
www.crabtreebooks.com

GET-INTO-IT GUIDES

Author: Vic Kovacs

Editors
Marcia Abramson, Philip Gebhardt, Janine Deschenes

Photo research
Pat B., Charlie Kompare, Melissa McClellan

Editorial director: Kathy Middleton

Proofreader: Wendy Scavuzzo

Cover/Interior Design: T.J. Choleva

**Production coordinator and
  Prepress technician:** Samara Parent

Print coordinator: Katherine Berti

Consultant: Joel Levin – co-founder of
TeacherGaming LLC, creators of MinecraftEdu,
with thanks to Eleanor Levin, age 10.

Photographs

Shutterstock.com: © sashahaltam (cover boy); © VGstockstudio (cover girl); © Pabkov (cover right, p. 4 left, 28 top right); © tovovan (Title page background); © Bloomua (p. 4 middle); © Ravennka (p. 5 bottom, 6 bottom, 10 bottom, 11 bottom, 13 bottom, 21 bottom, 25 bottom);
© urbanbuzz (p. 6 left); Creative Commons: Marco Verch (p. 4 right); Official GDC (p. 5 middle); © Gelpi JM (p. 6 middle);
© Austen Photogrpahy (p. 28-29); © Sam Taylor (p. 29 bottom right)

All screenshots for criticism and review. Minecraft®™ & © 2009–2016 Mojang/Notch

Developed and produced for Crabtree Publishing by BlueApple*Works* Inc.

Library and Archives Canada Cataloguing in Publication

Kovacs, Vic, author
        Get into Minecraft / Vic Kovacs.

(Get-into-it guides)
Includes index.
Issued in print and electronic formats.
ISBN 978-0-7787-2642-5 (hardback).--ISBN 978-0-7787-2648-7 (paperback).--ISBN 978-1-4271-1793-9 (html)

        1. Minecraft (Game)--Juvenile literature. I. Title.

GV1469.35.M535K68 2016   j794.8   C2016-903395-3
                                                              C2016-903396-1

Library of Congress Cataloging-in-Publication Data

Names: Kovacs, Vic, author.
Title: Get into Minecraft / Vic Kovacs.
Description: New York : Crabtree Publishing Company, [2016] | Series: Get-into-it guides | Includes index. |
  Audience: Ages: 8-11. | Audience: Grades: 4 to 6.
Identifiers: LCCN 2016026910 (print) | LCCN 2016031537 (ebook) | ISBN 9780778726425 (Reinforced library binding : alk. paper) | ISBN 9780778726487 (Paperback : alk. paper) | ISBN 9781427117939 (Electronic HTML)
Subjects: LCSH: Minecraft (Game)--Juvenile literature.
Classification: LCC GV1469.35.M535 K69 2016 (print) | LCC GV1469.35.M535 (ebook) | DDC 794.8--dc23
LC record available at https://lccn.loc.gov/2016026910

Crabtree Publishing Company
www.crabtreebooks.com   1-800-387-7650

Printed in Canada/072016/EF20160630

Published in Canada
Crabtree Publishing
616 Welland Ave.
St. Catharines, Ontario
L2M 5V6

Published in the United States
Crabtree Publishing
PMB 59051
350 Fifth Avenue, 59th Floor
New York, New York 10118

Published in the United Kingdom
Crabtree Publishing
Maritime House
Basin Road North, Hove
BN41 1WR

Published in Australia
Crabtree Publishing
3 Charles Street
Coburg North
VIC, 3058

CONTENTS

WORLD'S FAVORITE GAME

The first version of Minecraft was released in 2009 by its creator, the Swedish game designer and programmer Markus Persson. Throughout its development, its popularity exploded. Today, it's one of the best-selling video games of all time. With 100 million registered players, it is a true global phenomenon.

Minecraft takes place in a world made of building blocks. It is a **sandbox game**, which means players choose their own adventure. It can be played alone or with a group online. In Minecraft, there are no rules to say what a player can and can't do. Users are free to wander the wide open world, gathering **resources**, and using those resources to build shelters, monuments, and more.

Follow Internet safety rules and get permission from your parents before joining any online group. You want to stay safe in the world of Minecraft, just as you do in the real world.

The Minecraft World

Minecraft takes place in a **virtual** world where the sun rises and sets, and where snow and rain fall. You must build shelter and find food as you explore forests, mountains, oceans, mines, villages, dungeons, and many other locations. Nights are dangerous because monsters appear!

Every Minecraft game starts in the Overworld. It has so many types of environments that you may spend most of the game there.

You can stick to the relative safety of the Overworld—the main world of Minecraft—or you can venture into the lava-filled Nether and do battle with monsters! There's also the End, which is a **dimension** in outer space. The End is where you can fight the legendary Ender Dragon, which is the closest Minecraft comes to having a final boss.

The more you do, the more experience points you earn. Experience points are small, glowing orbs that allow you to move to a higher level and to do even more!

Notch

Markus Persson, also known as Notch (shown on the left), is the creator of Minecraft. He began developing the game in 2009. At first, he worked alone. Eventually, early versions of the game became so popular that he was able to quit his other jobs as a game **developer** and programmer to focus completely on his own creation. He started a company he called Mojang and hired other employees to help with the workload. At first, Notch's plan was to sell enough copies of Minecraft to finance future projects. However, the game was hugely successful and Mojang was bought by Microsoft in 2014 for $2.5 billion. It goes to show that if you believe in your own abilities, sometimes it pays off beyond your wildest dreams.

CHOOSE YOUR COMFORT ZONE

There are two main modes of play in Minecraft: Survival Mode and Creative Mode. Survival Mode is what most people think of when they think of Minecraft. In this mode, you gather resources and build things, but you also make weapons and **armor** to fight monsters. You also have to keep an eye on your health bar, and eat food to fill up your hunger bar. If fighting monsters, exploring, and collecting resources sounds fun, Survival is the mode to play.

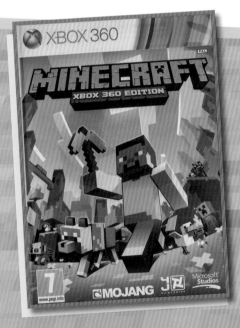

Minecraft Xbox 360 is one of the most popular versions of the game.

PLENTY OF WAYS TO PLAY

Originally developed for PCs, Minecraft is now available on a number of platforms. It's playable on computers running Windows or OS X (on Macs), and even the Linux operating system. There's the Pocket version, which can be played on Apple or Android devices such as smartphones and tablets, as well as on Windows phones. Then there are the console versions for the PlayStation 4, Xbox One, and WiiU. There's even a version for the PlayStation Vita handheld. PS3 and XBox 360 versions are also available. Basically, if there's a gadget in your home, you can probably play Minecraft on it!

CREATIVE MODE

In Creative Mode, you don't have to worry about staying alive. You can't die, and you start with access to unlimited building blocks. You also have the ability to fly. As a result, it is much easier to build massive, impressive structures in Creative Mode. There is no need to mine or explore, and you can begin creating things immediately. If you're mostly interested in playing Minecraft to build whatever you can imagine, Creative is probably the mode for you. It offers a peaceful, stress-free environment in which you can do just that. Creative Mode is like a giant canvas that's waiting for you to fill it with your own creations. You can spend as much time as you like building whatever you want, without pesky interruptions from monsters trying to kill you.

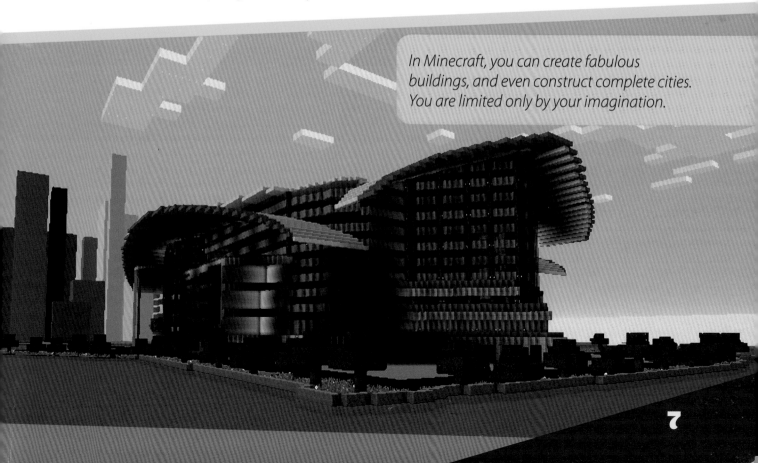

In Minecraft, you can create fabulous buildings, and even construct complete cities. You are limited only by your imagination.

WHAT TO EXPECT IN THE MINECRAFT WORLD

In Survival Mode, your immediate goal is (you guessed it!) to survive. To do that, you must find and gather the resources you need. You'll find the necessary resources in separate locations called environments. Knowing what you need and where to find it is a big part of the game. Because Minecraft's environment is randomly generated, you must be highly aware of your surroundings. For example, to build your first shelter, you could use wood, which you get from trees. Finding a forest would be a great start. In Creative Mode, you don't have to worry about surviving, so you can get right to building things.

Jungle Biomes may have River Biomes running through them. If you get lost in the jungle, you can craft a boat and follow the river out.

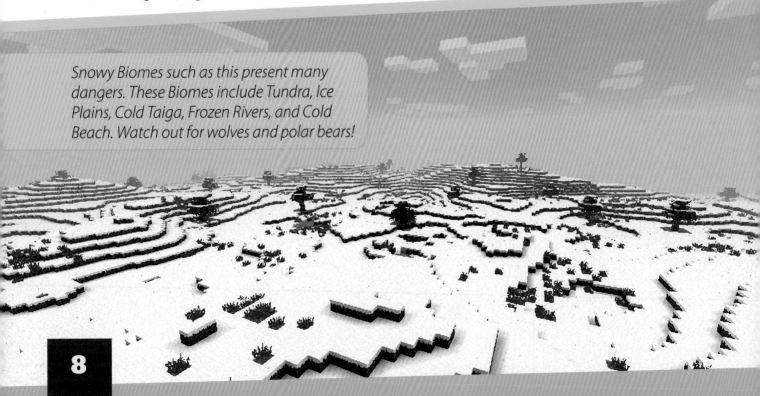

Snowy Biomes such as this present many dangers. These Biomes include Tundra, Ice Plains, Cold Taiga, Frozen Rivers, and Cold Beach. Watch out for wolves and polar bears!

BIOMES

The part of the game you start out in is called the Overworld. In the Overworld, there are many environments, called **Biomes**. The Overworld extends almost endlessly in all directions, and also has **portals** to other dimensions such as the Nether. A few of the more common Biomes found in the Overworld are:

The bright green Forests may contain mushrooms and flowers—but also enemies.

○ Forests filled with trees which can be turned into wood

○ Flat Plains with different types of grasses and flowers

○ Deserts and **Mesas** which are both home to various kinds of sands and clays

Villages and water sources often can be found in Flat Plains, along with horses and donkeys.

○ Extreme Hills which almost resemble mountains, and are the only place in the game where emeralds can be found

○ Jungles with giant trees and unique foods such as cocoa pods and melons

Many other Biomes can be found, but part of the fun is coming across them yourself!

Mesas are a somewhat rare but useful Biome. The red sand can be used to make glass. Clay can be used to make bricks.

Extreme Hills contain steep cliffs, mountains, waterfalls, and caverns. You risk falling and even dying when you venture into Extreme Hills.

MINING AND CRAFTING

To build anything in Survival Mode, you'll first need to gather resources. Some resources, such as wood from trees, can be found fairly easily above ground in Overworld. Others, such as minerals and **ores**, are found underground and need to be **mined**. Stone, dirt, and clay are common. Others, such as gold, **diamonds**, and emeralds, are much rarer.

MINECRAFT FACT – BLOCKS

Blocks are the basic building pieces of Minecraft. There are more than 100 different blocks, from air to yellow wool. Players must learn what each block does, how to get it, and how best to use it.

MINING TOOLS

To do any serious mining, you will need tools. At first, you'll only be able to make basic wooden versions. As you explore and gather more resources, you'll also be able to make more durable versions of tools using stone, as well as more exotic materials such as gold and diamond. The three basic tools are a pickaxe for mining, a shovel for digging, and an ax for chopping.

Pickaxes are vital for mining blocks and can also be used as a weapon.

Axes are used to collect wood more quickly. They also can be weapons.

Shovels help you pick up materials such as dirt and sand more easily.

CRAFTING

Crafting is just as important as mining in Minecraft. That's why the two were combined into its name. There are all kinds of instructions explaining how to make items from the many different resources you collect.

To make anything, you'll first have to build the Crafting Table, though. This is the item that you build most of your other items on. You'll also eventually build a furnace to **smelt** ore and produce charcoal, a brewing stand which can make potions, an anvil which lets you repair broken tools, and an enchantment table which powers up your equipment with special abilities!

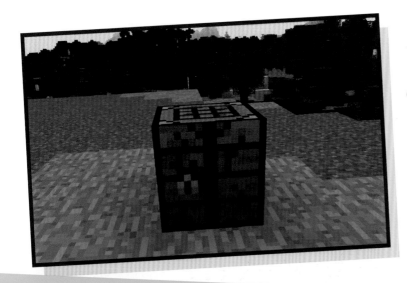

The Crafting Table was called Workbench in older versions of Minecraft.

A chest can hold 1,728 blocks.

CHEST

One of the first things you'll want to build is a **chest**. Chests are extremely useful. The chest allows you to store your items instead of keeping them in your **inventory**. This is important, because if you die, you may lose everything you're holding at the time. Anything kept in a chest can be retrieved after you **respawn**, though, which means you don't have to gather things all over again.

The Minecraft world is packed with different types of characters. You will meet villagers, animals, and supernatural characters such as witches and zombies. Called **mobs**, there are two main types in the game. The first are peaceful mobs, which do not attack you. They are also a good source of useful resources. Hostile mobs are the other main type of characters in Minecraft. These are what you might think of as enemies.

VILLAGERS

The peaceful villagers have five basic professions that are shown by the color of their robes. A farmer wears brown, a priest purple, and a librarian white. A blacksmith has a black apron and a butcher a white apron. Each profession offers different items in trade.

Robe color tells the basic profession of villagers, but they also can specialize. A farmer, for example, could be a shepherd.

Villagers buy and sell items ranging from food to ore to books, depending on their profession. They use emeralds as currency. Emeralds can be mined or found, but they are rare, so it is easier to trade for them.

Build pens so you can keep animals and collect food from them.

ANIMALS

There are many types of animals in Minecraft. Some, such as bats, are purely for show and have no greater purpose. Others, when killed, offer valuable **drops**. Chickens drop feathers, which can be used for arrows. Cows drop leather, which can be turned into clothing. Ocelots and wolves don't have any drops, but can be tamed. Once tamed, they turn into pet cats or dogs who can then follow you and assist you.

Animals also often drop raw meat which can be cooked and eaten. Meat is necessary to regain health and stay alive in the Survival Mode.

MINECRAFT FACT – HEALTH

As in real life, Minecraft players need to eat right and stay healthy. Two kinds of monitors (right) track how players are doing. The health monitor has a row of 10 hearts. The hunger monitor has 10 drumsticks. The symbols begin disappearing if players are hurt or hungry. Losing hearts and drumsticks makes the game more difficult.

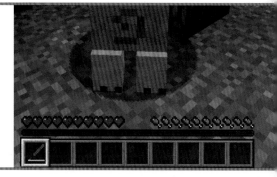

If you give a pair of sheep some wheat, they will produce a lamb.

SHEEP

Sheep are one of the most valuable mobs in the game. They drop wool which you need to build a bed. A bed allows you to sleep through the night. It also acts as a respawn point, in case you die. A sheep can be killed to obtain its wool, but it can also be sheared, which keeps the sheep alive. Shearing provides more wool than killing the sheep would. Wool can also be dyed a variety of colors.

13

HOSTILE MOBS

You need to watch out for hostile mobs and know what each one is capable of doing. If they see you, they will usually attack. Combat is sometimes beneficial since hostile mobs often leave useful drops after they are killed.

SKELETONS

This mob attacks from a distance using bows and arrows. It's better to fight them from a distance using a bow. Getting too close can be very dangerous. They drop arrows and bones.

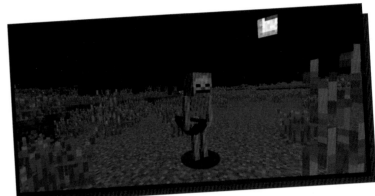

ZOMBIES

*Appearing in groups of four, this mob will attack and chase after you. They continue to attack even when injured. Any weapon is effective against a zombie, including swords and arrows. They drop rotten flesh when killed, and very rarely, **ingots**, carrots, and potatoes.*

SPIDERS

Spiders often lie in wait before ambushing you. They will hide on the ceilings by climbing up the walls above an opening. They'll wait for you and drop down when you walk under them. They drop string and spider eyes.

CREEPERS

Very dangerous mobs, they usually sneak up on you from behind. Once within your range, a creeper will hiss and begin to flash. They then explode. Hitting them with arrows before they get close enough to blow up is usually the best strategy. You can also hit them with a sword and retreat, but that is risky. They drop gunpowder or music discs, when killed by a skeleton's arrow.

ENDERMAN

This mob hates it when you look at them. They will attack if you look directly at them. They can teleport, and your best strategy is to just leave them alone. If you don't attack or stare at them, they won't attack you. If you need to fight them, they are vulnerable to elements such as fire and water. A bucket of water is your most effective tool against them. They drop Ender Pearls after being killed.

ENDER DRAGON

The Ender Dragon swoops down and charges at you. It can heal itself, so it is tough to defeat! You need to use your best weapons. Defeating it activates the exit portal.

YOUR FIRST DAY IN THE MINECRAFT WORLD

Now that you know what you're getting into, it's time to start playing and making your own fun! The first choice is between Survival and Creative Modes. If you choose Survival, you'll appear (or **spawn**) in a random location. Sometimes you'll be lucky enough to spawn close to the resources you need. Other times, you'll have to do some exploring to find them. The most important task to complete on your first day is to build a basic shelter. You must do this before nightfall. If you don't, you'll be vulnerable to attack from hostile mobs. Days only last 10 minutes in real time, so you'll have to act quickly.

Minecraft's 20-minute day-night cycle starts as soon as you spawn. Daytime is followed by sunset, seven minutes of night, and sunrise. If you can't see the sky, a clock will help you keep alert to nighttime dangers. You can trade for a clock or craft one.

If you do not start out near a forest, you will need to find one quickly to be able to build a wooden shelter. If you don't find a forest, build your first shelter out of dirt.

Starting Out

When you start out, you'll have no tools. This means, to gather the wood you need to build a shelter, you'll have to punch trees down with YOUR BARE HANDS! Once you gather enough blocks of wood, you will need to build the Crafting Table. With a Crafting Table, you can build more complex items and tools.

As soon as you have enough wood, make sure to build the Crafting Table. This is the surface you'll use to make all your tools and items.

As well as wood, you will want to gather some **cobblestone** blocks. The cobblestone will allow you to build a furnace once you've made your shelter. The furnace can also turn wood into charcoal, which you can use to make torches. These can light your home and scare off hostile mobs, because mobs do not like light.

MINECRAFT FACT – CRAFTING TABLE

It takes four planks of wood of any kind to make the Crafting Table. Sometimes they occur naturally in libraries, witch huts, and igloos, but Crafting Tables are so important that it's best not to wait to find one.

Besides building a shelter, you should also get food on your first day. Keep an eye out for fruit on trees, and animals such as cows. You can whack them for a food drop.

Once you have the resources you need, you can build your first shelter. Some players find it easier to build into hills or underground, which eliminates the need to build walls. Remember to use a door at the entrance. Above ground or below, it's completely up to you! You decide exactly how you want to play the game.

THE FIRST NIGHT'S ADVENTURES

Once you have a shelter, you can settle in for the night and start building some things you'll need. Make sure you bring your Crafting Table into your new home. Using it, you can craft eight blocks of cobblestone into a furnace. Once you have the furnace, you can burn wood to make charcoal. Combine one stick and one piece of charcoal to make a torch. Make as many torches as you need to light your shelter. That way, you'll be able to see throughout the night. Next, make any tools you don't yet have, such as an ax, a pickax, and a shovel. A sword will also come in handy. You should also build your first chest using eight wooden planks. Any extra items you don't need should be placed in the chest to keep them safe.

During nighttime the world is covered in darkness and hostile mobs will spawn on the surface but you will be safe in your shelter.

If you build your first Crafting Table and furnace outside, remember to bring them inside when your shelter has been completed. You will be able to keep making torches and other useful items after night falls.

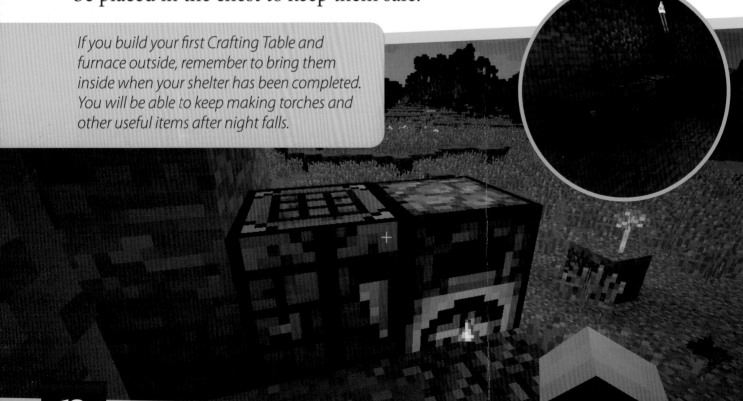

GOING MINING

Once you've constructed the basics, you can go on your first mining expedition. Dig down into the floor of your shelter in a staircase pattern. If you see valuable resources such as coal or iron, gather as much as you can. If you need to, return home and place them in your chest. You might even find an underground cavern rich in resources. Be careful, though! There are many hostile mobs that lurk underground.

Digging straight up or down can be dangerous. You should avoid it.

Coal

When you see a deposit of coal, get it. Be careful while digging because hostile mobs like to hide nearby.

MINECRAFT FACT – TORCHES

Light helps players stay safe in Minecraft, so torches play an important role. A torch can fend off hostile mobs, light up dangers at night, and help you find your way home. One thing they can't do is set things on fire.

Crafting

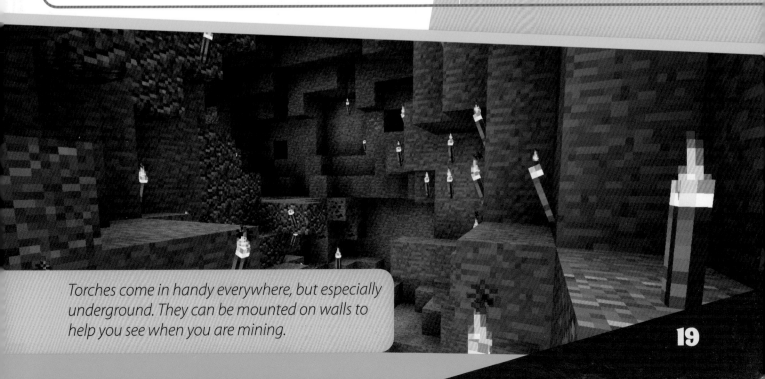

Torches come in handy everywhere, but especially underground. They can be mounted on walls to help you see when you are mining.

DAY TWO: IMPROVING YOUR SHELTER

Once the sun comes up on your second day, your main task should be making some improvements on your home base. Find sand, which can be used to make glass for windows. **Cacti** can be placed around your home for additional protection from hostile mobs. Also, gather as much wood as you can, since it is always useful. If you have a sword, this would be a great time to go hunting for food. If you encounter any sheep, not only will they drop raw mutton, they will also drop wool. Three wool and three wood planks can be used to craft a bed. This is an **essential** item for your home, so make it as soon as you can.

Sleeping in your bed at night keeps hostile mobs away. Your first night's sleep also sets your spawn point. If you lose your life, you will respawn in your shelter.

Wool comes in 16 colors. You can use wool of any color to make your bed. However, once the bed is produced, it will always end up being the same color.

If you decide to plant cacti for protection, do it very carefully. Cacti can harm or destroy anything that comes into contact with them, including you. You will lose half a heart if you touch a cactus.

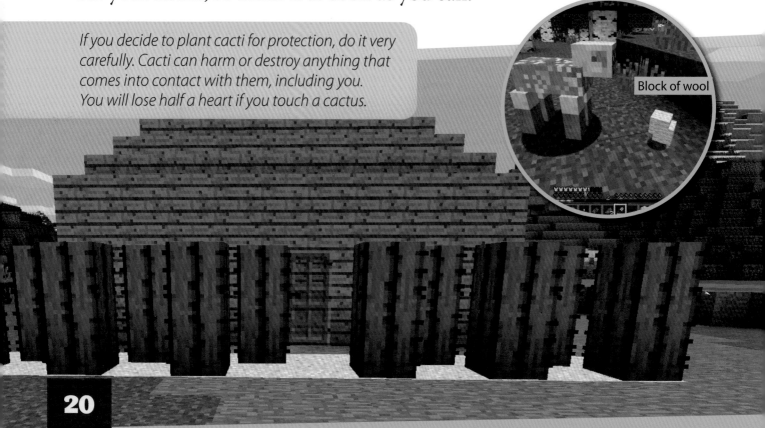

Block of wool

Sand can be used to make key items such as windows, but you can't make sand. Instead, it can be mined with a pickax or collected with a shovel.

Sand blocks

Windows can be crafted from glass blocks or panes, which give a better view outside. To make glass, you first need sand.

BUILDING IT UP

Once you arrive back home, you can use the furnace to make sand into glass blocks. Those can then be used to make glass panes for windows. If you built your first shelter underground, now would be a good time to raise walls using wooden planks. Try to place windows in all your walls, which will allow light in during the day. You can also use the furnace to cook any food you've picked up. Cooking increases the amount of energy you get from food. You can also build stronger tools out of minerals you've gathered. Stone tools and weapons are stronger than wooden ones. The same is true of other mined elements, such as iron and diamonds.

Armor

GEAR UP

The world of Minecraft can be dangerous when you're starting out. That's why it's important to protect yourself. You can make suits of armor out of leather, iron, gold, or diamond. Each suit is made up of a helmet, a chestplate, leggings, and boots. It takes 24 pieces of material to make an entire suit. You'll also need weapons, including a sword and a bow. You'll need to make arrows to fire from the bow. Once you have weapons, you will want to practice with them so you can be as effective as possible in battle. After all, there's no point in having a great bow if you can't hit anything with it.

21

PREPARE TO EXPLORE

Now that you have a good home base, it's time to head out into the world and see what you can find. It's important to prepare for a trip. You don't want to get into trouble that you could have avoided if you had brought the right item. Bring enough food to keep yourself healthy. Having enough wood and cobblestone to build a temporary shelter is smart. Having an abundance of dirt can also come in handy. For example, if you fall into a **chasm** you can't get out of, you can stack the dirt to escape. Make sure you have the equipment for the task you want to accomplish. For example, if you're planning on going mining, bring a pickax. A bed will also let you sleep through the night if you get stuck after dark in your temporary shelter.

Be extra careful when exploring caverns and ravines. Falling is not the only danger. Hostile mobs may be hiding there.

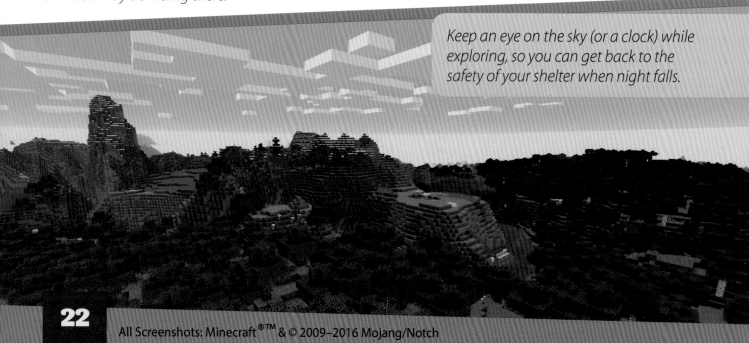

Keep an eye on the sky (or a clock) while exploring, so you can get back to the safety of your shelter when night falls.

Diamonds are just as precious in Minecraft as in the outside world. The shiny blue gems make the strongest armor and tools, but they are very rare. You may need to brave dangerous caves to mine diamonds, so bring lots of torches. A very lucky player may find a diamond hiding in a chest.

Diamonds

STAYING SAFE

There are also some steps to take to make sure you stay safe while exploring. First of all, wear armor. Second, stay aware of your surroundings. If you wander into lava or fall off a cliff and die, you'll drop all the items you went out to gather. You'll also want to take steps to make sure you don't get lost. There are two

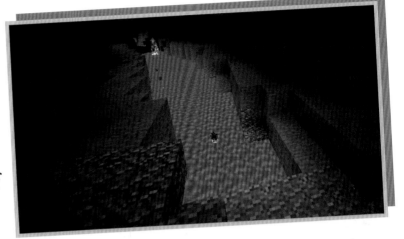

Lava will destroy items it touches, and it can kill you. Watch out for pools of lava when you are underground.

popular ways to mark your trail. One, you can place torches as you go. Two, you can leave tall towers that are easy to see. Once you want to return to your base, you just follow these markers all the way home.

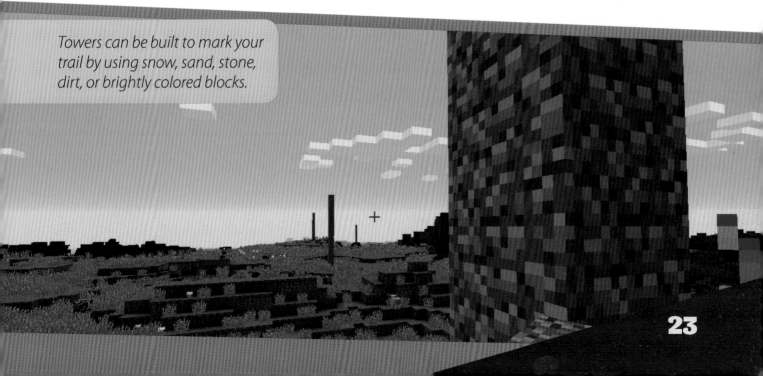

Towers can be built to mark your trail by using snow, sand, stone, dirt, or brightly colored blocks.

SETTLING IN

As you venture farther and farther into the world, you'll find a wider variety of resources. You can then use these resources to build a bigger house. You can also add improvements, such as a garden where you can grow your own crops. You can even make pens to raise your own animals for their drops. Once you've created a **foundation** for yourself, you're free to do whatever you want. Build a better house. Build a castle. Build anything you can imagine! There are no limits to what you can accomplish in Minecraft.

Your house can be simple, fancy, or even spooky. It's up to you.

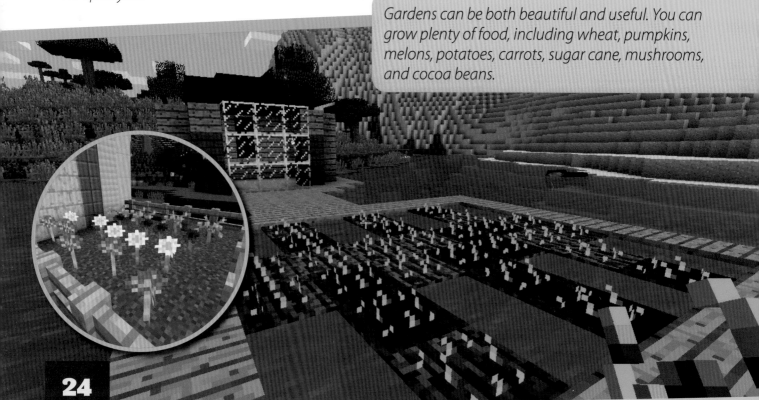

Gardens can be both beautiful and useful. You can grow plenty of food, including wheat, pumpkins, melons, potatoes, carrots, sugar cane, mushrooms, and cocoa beans.

RAISING YOUR OWN LIVESTOCK

Once you've built pens, you'll need to fill them with animals. Each animal has a favorite type of food. You can use this food to lure them into your pens. If you have at least two of the same type of animal, you can also feed them their favorite food to make them breed. Once given the food it likes, the animal will enter love mode. A heart will appear above the animal's head. If it's in range of another animal of the same species, they will appear to kiss. Once they separate, there will be a brand-new baby between them. This is a great way to ensure you have a steady supply of food close to home.

If you offer wheat to sheep and cows, carrots to pigs, and seeds to chickens, they will follow you home.

Cooked meats are the food that makes you the strongest, so it's a good idea to keep herds of pigs and cows.

HOUSEHOLD PETS

The same method you use to tame **livestock** can be used on wild wolves and ocelots. Ocelots love fish, and wolves love meat. Once you feed them, wolves will become tame dogs and ocelots will become tame cats. Pets will follow you around. They also have other uses: dogs can attack hostile mobs, and cats scare away creepers!

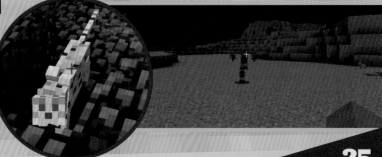

Wolves will get a red collar when they become dogs. Ocelots turn into tabby, tuxedo, or Siamese cats. Besides scaring the mobs away, pets will follow you around and you can make your pet dog sit and stay, or follow you on adventures.

BUILD YOUR OWN CREATIONS

Players around the world have used Minecraft to build some truly amazing projects. Users have built entire cities, famous starships, and even a working foosball table. Some players enjoy recreating parts of their favorite movies and books, while others prefer to build structures they dream up themselves. There are

More than 100,000 blocks were needed to create a Minecraft replica of Yankee Stadium.

entire groups of players who **collaborate** to build things bigger than they could accomplish on their own. Others prefer to create solo. There's no wrong way to play Minecraft, just like there's no wrong way to be creative.

This creation is a complete view of a space shuttle waiting to launch at a launch tower.

BUILD AND LEARN

Minecraft has also been used for science fair projects. Players have used the game to recreate historic buildings and cities. One user built an exact replica of China's Forbidden City! The game can also be used to explain mathematical concepts. You can use the game to build architectural models. The redstone can be used to create circuits, which in turn can be used to build complex machines.

Teachers can import historical models into the game and let students explore them. This allows history to come to life in previously impossible ways! There's even an entire edition of the game that was designed for use in the classroom. It's a great way to teach and learn a variety of subjects in a fun, engaging way.

minecraft beta 1.4_01

Minecraft projects come from science and history. They include working computers (above), and recreations of historical sites such as the Forbidden City—a vast palace in Beijing (below).

MINECRAFT PROJECT: CRAFT A SWORD

Steve is one of the main characters of Minecraft. Alex was added in later versions to represent female players. Steve and Alex act out a player's choices but they never talk. They can build complex structures all by themselves, and show great skill with a sword.

Make your own sword out of card stock. It is a fun craft that matches the skills required for the game. Just as cubes are the basic building units of Minecraft, card stock squares are the basic units of this craft.

STEPS TO MAKE THE BLADE

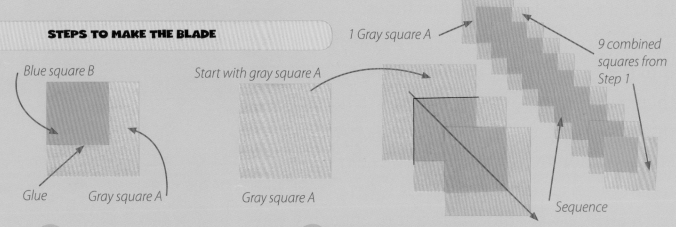

Blue square B

Glue   Gray square A

Start with gray square A

Gray square A

1 Gray square A

9 combined squares from Step 1

Sequence

1. Use the pattern below to trace and cut pieces as listed. Make nine combined squares by gluing blue square B to gray square A as shown above.

2. To make the blade, start with a gray square A. Glue combined squares from Step 1 onto the gray square A in a sequence as shown. Use a blue square B as a guide for placement. Continue layering the rest of the combined squares.

PATTERN AND MATERIALS

You Will Need

- gray card stock
- blue card stock
- brown card stock
- 12 gray squares A
- 9 blue squares B
- 2 gray squares B
- 7 blue squares C
- 3 brown squares C
- cardboard or foamboard

Square A

Square B

Square C

3 Cut one square C out of the corner of a gray square A as shown. Glue two blue squares C on as shown.

Cut away

Glue 2 squares

Glue

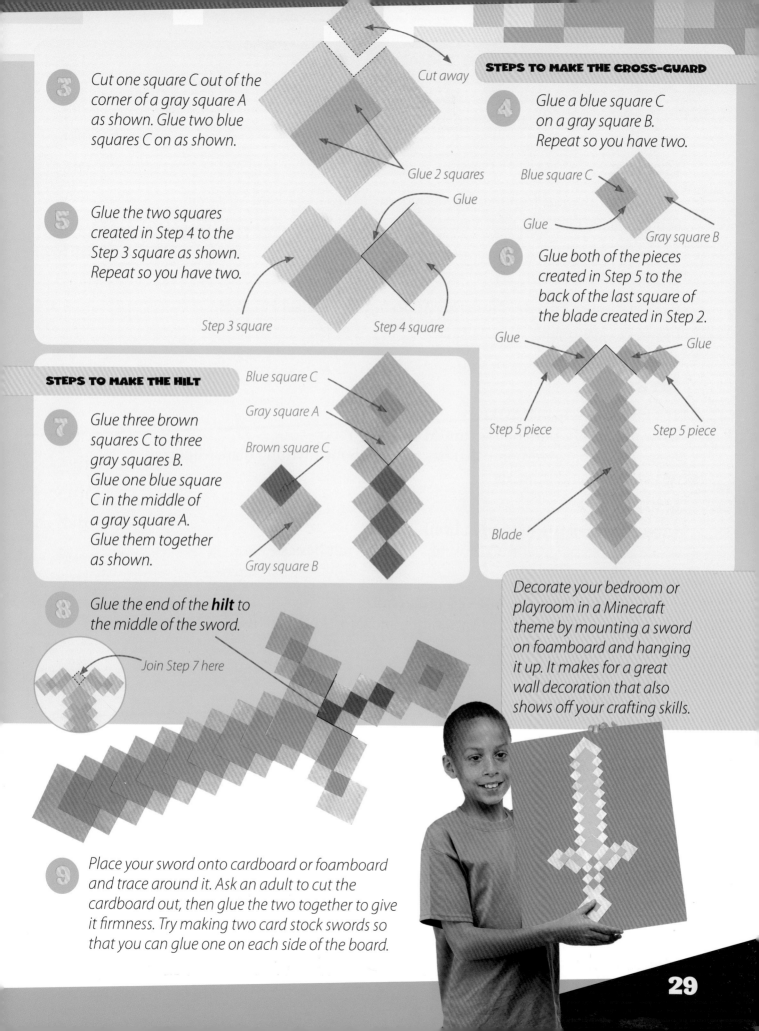

4 Glue a blue square C on a gray square B. Repeat so you have two.

Blue square C

Glue

Gray square B

5 Glue the two squares created in Step 4 to the Step 3 square as shown. Repeat so you have two.

Step 3 square

Step 4 square

6 Glue both of the pieces created in Step 5 to the back of the last square of the blade created in Step 2.

Glue

Glue

Step 5 piece

Step 5 piece

Blade

STEPS TO MAKE THE HILT

Blue square C

Gray square A

Brown square C

Gray square B

7 Glue three brown squares C to three gray squares B. Glue one blue square C in the middle of a gray square A. Glue them together as shown.

8 Glue the end of the **hilt** to the middle of the sword.

Join Step 7 here

Decorate your bedroom or playroom in a Minecraft theme by mounting a sword on foamboard and hanging it up. It makes for a great wall decoration that also shows off your crafting skills.

9 Place your sword onto cardboard or foamboard and trace around it. Ask an adult to cut the cardboard out, then glue the two together to give it firmness. Try making two card stock swords so that you can glue one on each side of the board.

29

LEARNING MORE

Books

Minecraft: Essential Handbook by Stephanie Milton and Paul Soares Jr., Scholastic, 2015

Master Builder Junior: Minecraft Secrets for Young Crafters by Triumph Books, Triumph Books, 2016

Build, Discover, Survive! Mastering Minecraft by Michael Lummis,

Prima Games, 2015

Websites

The Official Minecraft Wiki
www.minecraft.gamepedia.com/Minecraft_Wiki
A great searchable resource that has articles about anything that's Minecraft-related you could think of

Minecraft 101
www.minecraft101.net/index.html
A site with some great walkthroughs of Minecraft basics

GameFAQs
www.gamefaqs.com/pc/606524-minecraft/
A site with walkthroughs, cheats, hints, and a forum where users can ask questions about the game

minecraft.net
www.minecraft.net/
The game's official site, with basic info on the game and links to community resources

education.minecraft.net
http://education.minecraft.net
Minecraft: Education Edition is an open-world game for educators, administrators, and students that promotes creativity, collaboration, and problem solving.

GLOSSARY

armor Protective clothing

Biomes The different types of environments in Minecraft

cacti The plural form of cactus; thorny plants usually found in the desert

chasm A deep hole or opening in a surface, especially the surface of a planet

chest A type of box used to store items

cobblestones Small stones that were once used to pave streets

collaborate Team up to work together

developer A person who designs and builds video games

diamond A very strong type of gemstone

dimension A large area in Minecraft, such as the Overworld

drop An item that appears in Minecraft when something dies or in certain other circumstances

essential Absolutely necessary

foundation A base layer that other things are built on

hilt A handle of a weapon or tool, especially a sword, dagger, or knife

ingot A piece of metal that has been formed into a particular shape such as a brick

inventory All the things that a player acquires; also a name for the pop-up menu that players use to manage items

livestock Animals raised to provide food or other goods, like milk or leather

mesa A hill or plateau with a flat top and steep sides

mine The act of digging underground for the purpose of gathering resources

mob Non-player creatures in Minecraft

ore Mineral blocks that can be smelted into resources

portal A structure that allows a player to travel to another dimension

resources The various types of materials the player can gather to build things with

respawn Reappear and be placed back in the game after dying

sandbox game An open-world or free-roaming game, named for the way kids play in a sandbox

smelt Produce goods using a furnace in Minecraft

spawn To be created and placed into the game

virtual Existing or happening on computers or the Internet

INDEX